JAN 2012

FOR JOSH & JAKE —

THIS BOOK WILL HELP

YOU TO LEARN SOME OF

THE BIRDS — SO NEXT

TIME WE GO TO NISQUALLY

DELTA WE CAN IDENTIFY

THEM TOGETHER !!

LOVE,
COOPER & CODY

Alphabet Bird Collection

Text and illustrations by Shelli Ogilvy

SASQUATCH BOOKS
SEATTLE

Avocet

With long legs and a slender bill,
The Avocet wades through water with skill.

American Avocets live near marshes, ponds, and mud flats. Sweeping a long bill back and forth underwater, they hunt for insects and bugs. At times groups of one hundred birds can be observed feeding together.

Sing along to the Avocet's song:

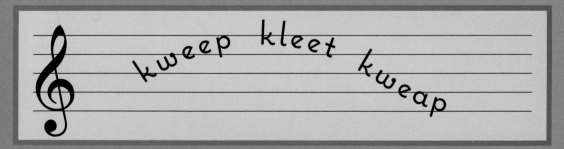

Brant

Summers in the Arctic and winters on southern shores,
Fast and far the Brant soars.

Brants migrate north to breed and nest on Arctic tundra. They often fly in flocks of twenty to thirty birds. During migration brants can be heard aloft from a far distance.

Sing along to the Brant's song:

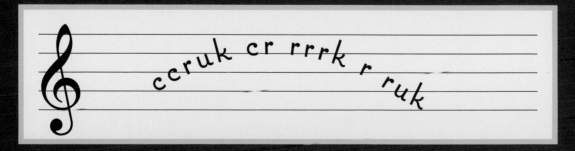

Crane

Through song and dance,
The Crane finds romance.

The **Sandhill Crane** is found throughout western North America. In spring large groups of male cranes display a joyful dance for the females. Cranes often fly high over-head. Their distinctive call places them in the sky even when they are above the clouds.

Sing along to the Crane's song:

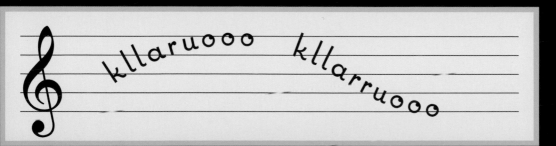

Dove

Graceful and white,
A Dove takes flight.

Easily adaptable to new environments, **Doves** are present almost everywhere on earth. They are strong fliers, moving with grace and agility through the air. Doves are considered a symbol of peace, and their soothing call brings tranquility.

Sing along to the Dove's song:

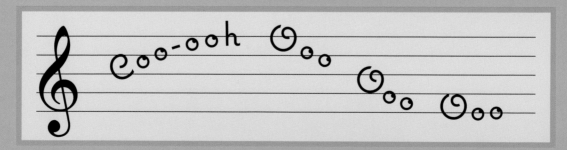

Eagle

From high on the limb of a tree,
The Eagle looks out to sea.

The **Bald Eagle** is the national bird and symbol of the United States. It acquires its white head when it is three to five years old. Perching on cliffs or branches above seacoasts, rivers, and lakes, eagles readily spy a fresh meal below. Their high-pitched call can be heard year-round.

Sing along to the Eagle's song:

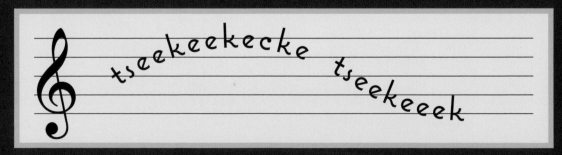

tseekeekecke tseekeeek

flicker

The Flicker searches for insects and seeds,
And with a long tongue it feeds.

Northern Flickers are a type of woodpecker. Their long tongues allow them to hunt for insects and ants on the ground, in tree bark, or even under the siding of houses. Their loud calls and bright underwings make them easy to recognize.

Sing along to the Flicker's song:

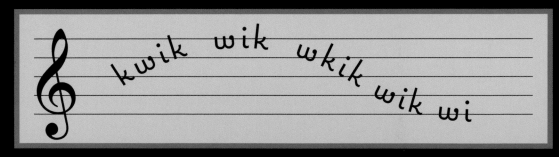

Gull

Above lakes and ocean beaches Gulls fly,
Laughing and making a noisy cry.

Gulls or seagulls are most often encountered near water. They mix in large groups, landing and taking off in unison. Some gulls nest on rocky cliffs, while others make a small depression on the beach just above the water's edge.

Sing along to the Gull's song:

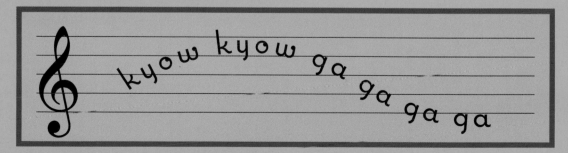

H

Heron

Quietly walking in shallow bogs,
A Heron hunts for fish and frogs.

Great Blue Herons are graceful wading birds.
Standing still on the shore, they pierce the water with a
long bill in search of food. In flight their neck curves
inward and their large wings beat slowly. Though silent
while hunting, if surprised the heron utters a most
ungraceful sound.

Sing along to the Heron's song:

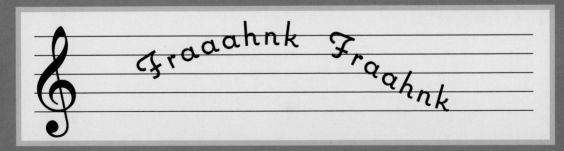

Ibis

At sunrise a flock of Ibises fly,
Like an ivory cloud in the sky.

The **White Ibis** is found in coastal areas of the southern United States and the Caribbean. As the sun rises or sets, large flocks are seen gliding through the air, returning to their roost.

Sing along to the Ibis's song:

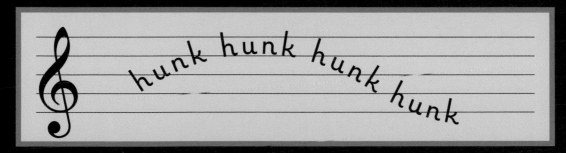

Junco

Twigs and grasses make the nest,
In which the Junco can rest.

Dark-eyed Juncos are commonly seen at bird feeders in winter; other times of the year they feed on insects and berries. Their small nests, which bear many young over the summer, are found in open woodlands and meadows. Their song fills the air in wild or urban lands.

Sing along to the Junco's song:

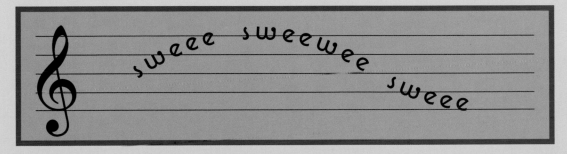

Kingfisher

Diving from the air in quick pursuit,
The Kingfisher hunts for fish or maybe a newt.

The **Belted Kingfisher** is found in many waterside areas of North America. Kingfishers are swift hunters, diving headfirst into the water. They aggressively defend their territory, making loud, rattling calls to send other birds away.

Sing along to the Kingfisher's song:

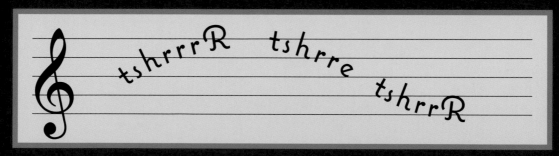

L Loon

From the calm surface of the lake,
Gracefully a Loon dives without a wake.

Common Loons are incredible divers: they can plunge up to 150 feet deep. They feed mainly on fish—most are swallowed underwater. Their haunting call can be heard echoing on many northern lakes and bays.

Sing along to the Loon's song:

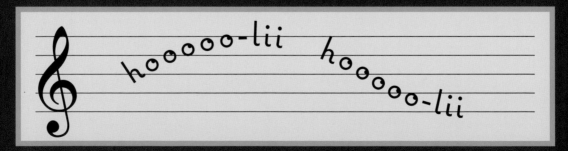

Magpie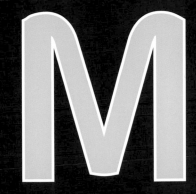

Mischievous and strikingly loud,
A group of Magpies makes a noisy crowd.

The **Black-billed Magpie** resides throughout the western United States. In winter months it is often one of the few birds around. Magpies have a reputation for playfulness and making raucous noise at all times of day.

Sing along to the Magpie's song:

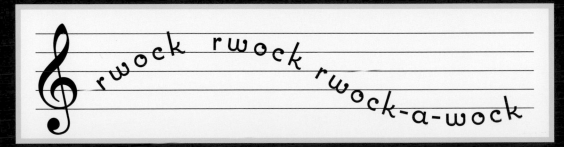

Nighthawk

At dusk you might see from under the eve,
Nighthawks hunting, as they bob and weave.

In the evening **Common Nighthawks** come out to feed.
Their large mouths and flying acrobatics can be confused
with those of bats. However, their soft call identifies this
bird rather than other insect hunters.

Sing along to the Nighthawk's song:

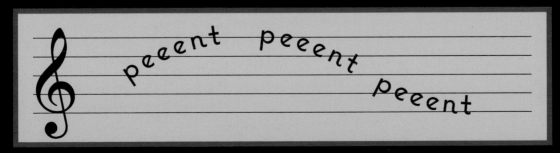

O Oystercatcher

The Oystercatcher runs and bustles,
Prying open a meal of mussels.

Black Oystercatchers are most often sighted on the west coast of North America. Their strong chisel-shaped bill is ideal for prying open mussels, clams, and other shellfish. They build their nest on the shore slightly above the highest tide line. Their brash and bold vocal sounds will alert any intruder wandering too close.

Sing along to the Oystercatcher's song:

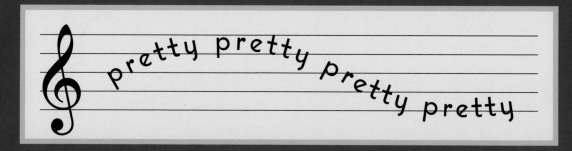

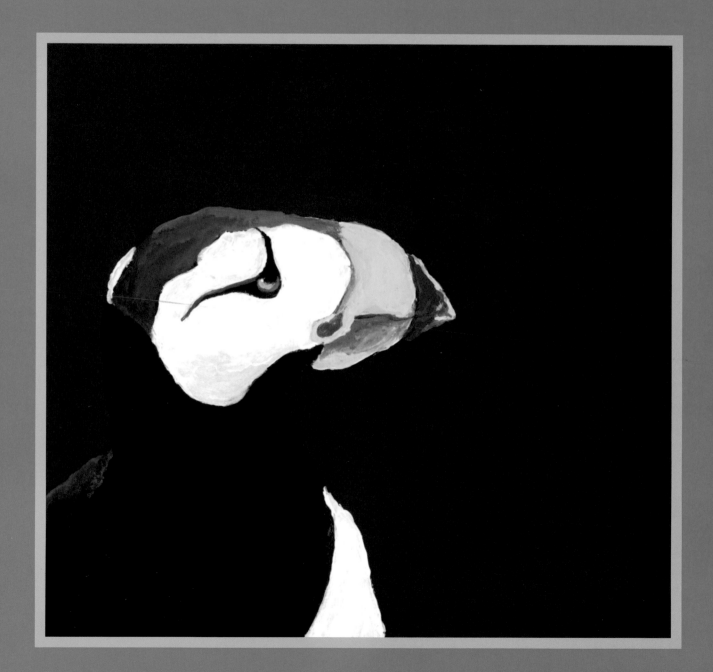

Puffin

In all kinds of weather,
Puffins nest together.

Puffins effortlessly dive for fish in cold ocean waters.
Dense feathers and strong wings allow them to stay
underwater for long periods of time. They nest on sod–
covered islands in large colonies. Although they are not
a noisy group, sometimes a soft utter can be heard.

Sing along to the Puffin's song:

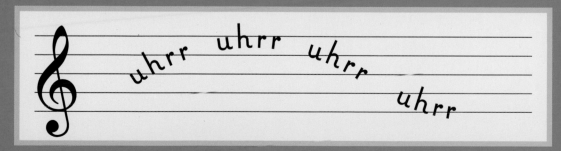

 Quetzal

In a Guatemalan forest's early morning light,
Spy a Quetzal, colorful and bright.

The **Resplendent Quetzal** is the national bird of Guatemala. Its long tail feathers serve as camouflage for its nest. Though it is not a strong flier, it is able to move from tree to tree, devouring a bounty of fruit at each stop.

Sing along to the Quetzal's song:

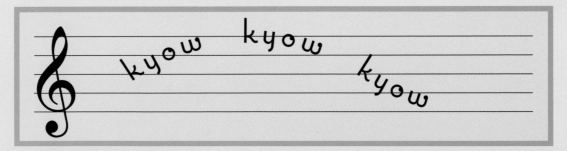

Raven

Playful and cunning,
The speech of the Raven is stunning.

Ravens are known for their crafty intelligence and ability to flourish in many different habitats. They are apt scavengers, reserving time for mischief and play. The raven is believed to be a magical creature in many cultures. Its varied speech has even inspired poetry.

Sing along to the Raven's song:

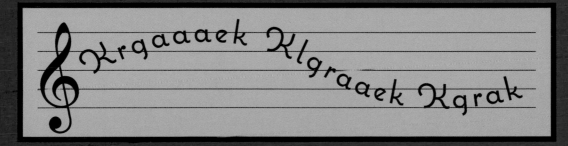

Swallow

On warm currents of air,
Swallows chase insects with flair.

Barn Swallows are familiar in North America as well as Europe. They spend more time aloft than most other birds. Swallows feed primarily in flight, their main food source being flying insects. They nest under bridges or in the eaves of buildings, and are easily heard chattering as they feed and fledge their young.

Sing along to the Swallow's song:

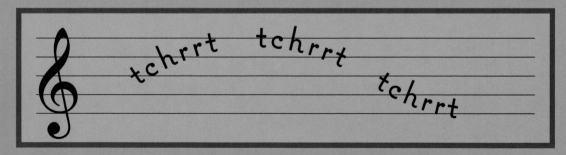

T Tern

Traveling 22,000 miles a year,
Arctic Terns fly in both hemispheres.

Arctic Terns fly tremendous distances in a year. In summer months they are found nesting in the Northern Hemisphere; as the seasons change the birds travel south in search of food. Many will spend the winter months as far south as Antarctica.

Sing along to the Tern's song:

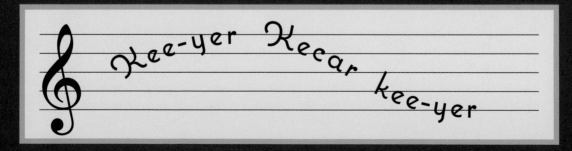

Kee-yer Kecar kee-yer

 Upland Sandpiper

Chasing crickets out on the plain,
The Upland Sandpiper sings even in rain.

Upland Sandpipers dwell in grasslands, meadows, and open fields. They eat crickets, grasshoppers, and various other insects. Their sweet sound can be heard in flight or on the ground in many Midwestern states.

Sing along to the Upland Sandpiper's song:

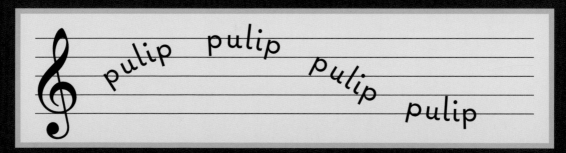

Varied Thrush

Out of the forest and brush,
Rings a note from the Varied Thrush.

In the northwest United States, the **Varied Thrush** thrives. A distinguishing splash of orange reveals its location in dense vegetation. It feeds on insects, spiders, berries, and seeds. Its song fills damp forest air, dense thickets, and brush.

Sing along to the Varied Thrush's song:

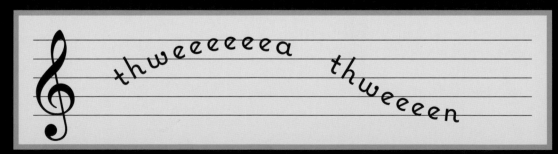

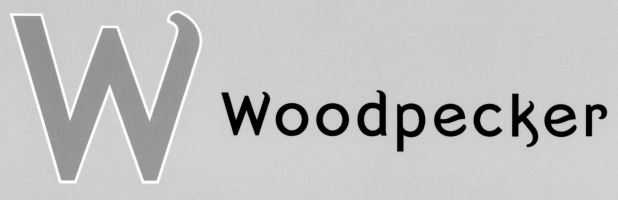

W Woodpecker

Drilling holes in the bark of trees,
The Woodpecker's tongue finds insects and bees.

The **Pileated Woodpecker** makes a hole in the bark of trees in search of beetles, ants, and other insects. Loud drilling sounds echo throughout woodlands in the southeast United States. The woodpecker's call can be heard as it flies to feed its young.

Sing along to the Woodpecker's song:

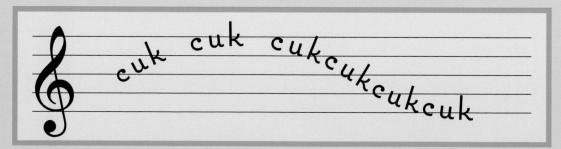

cuk cuk cukcukcukcuk

Xantus's Murrelet

Far out at sea and rarely seen from the beach,
The Xantus's Murrelet can seem out of reach.

Murrelets are sturdy swimmers, propelling underwater with strong wingbeats. The **Xantus's Murrelet** nests on offshore islands. When chicks are just two days old they go out to sea, following their parents' cries.

Sing along to the Xantus's Murrelet's song:

Yellowthroat Y

Camouflaged in bushes and weeds,
The Yellowthroat sings as it hunts for seeds.

The **Common Yellowthroat** hides from predators in grasses, thickets, and marshes. It feeds primarily on insects, spiders, and seeds. It is often hard to see, but a spirited call gives away this small bird.

Sing along to the Yellowthroat's song:

Z

Zone-tailed Hawk

The Zone-tailed Hawk soars over marshes and lakes,
Searching for a meal of lizards and snakes.

Zone-tailed Hawks are high-soaring birds. With their wings shaped in a V, they climb to great heights on warm currents of air. Their piercing call sounds similar to the much more common Red-tailed Hawk.

Sing along to the Zone-tailed Hawk's song:

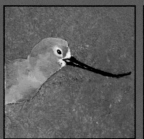

Avocet

Brant

Crane

Dove

Eagle

Junco

Kingfisher

Loon

Magpie

Raven

Swallow

Tern

Upland
Sandpiper

Flicker

Gull

Heron

Ibis

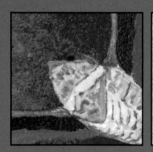
Nighthawk

Oystercatcher

Puffin

Quetzal

Varied Thrush

Woodpecker

Xantus's
Murrelet

Yellowthroat

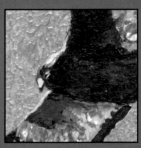
Zone-tailed Hawk

To all the friends and family that supported the idea
of this book and endured many a bird-call translation.
And to all present and future bird lovers.

Printed in China
Published by Sasquatch Books
Distributed by PGW/Perseus
15 14 13 12 11 10 09   9 8 7 6 5 4 3 2 1

Cover illustration: Shelli Ogilvy
Cover design: Sasquatch Books/Gretchen Scoble
Author photograph: Shelli Ogilvy
Interior illustrations: Shelli Ogilvy
Interior design and composition: Gretchen Scoble

Library of Congress Cataloging-in-Publication Data

Ogilvy, Shelli.
  Alphabet bird collection / text and illustrations by Shelli Ogilvy.
    p. cm.
  Includes index.
  ISBN-13: 978-1-57061-618-1
  ISBN-10: 1-57061-618-3
  1. Ornithological illustration. 2. Birds--Identification. 3. Birds in art. 4. Alphabet books. I. Title.
  QL674.4.O35 2009
  598--dc22

                    2009017123

Sasquatch Books
119 South Main Street, Suite 400
Seattle, WA 98104
(206) 467-4300
www.sasquatchbooks.com
custserv@sasquatchbooks.com